# SOUVENIR PICTURE GUIDE
# THE BROADS

# SALMON BOOKS

# THE BROADS

The largest protected wetland in the British Isles, the beautiful Broads are made up of over 120 miles of gentle waterways and attract nearly two million visitors each year. This unique combination of rivers, lakes, marshes and fens, dotted with pretty villages and historic market towns, offers excellent sailing and cruising, and the opportunity to watch the diversity of wildlife which is found there. The Broads were created in part through the silting up of the river mouths which caused the streams to flow more slowly and widen out into shallow meres. The digging of peat for fuel also played a part in the process. For many hundreds of years, considerable quantities of peat were taken from the area until, some five or six hundred years ago, the diggings began to flood, creating the reed-fringed lakes we see today. The area is cared for and managed by the Broads Authority, which was established in 1989 and given the huge task of restoring the Broads after years of neglect had left the water clouded and the fens turning to shrubland.

Norfolk Wherry at South Walsham

Photo: tournorfolk.co.uk

The distinctive wherries, with the traditional black sails on a hinged mast which could be lowered to pass beneath the numerous bridges, carried cargoes along the network of Broadland rivers. Although the last wherry was built in 1912, they continued to work on the Broads up to the Second World War. Today, a handful of these unique boats have been preserved and are used as pleaasure boats.

Sailing on the River Ant

Pleasure Boat Dyke, Hickling

# BROADLAND WILDLIFE

The shallow lakes, or broads, connected by an intricate network of rivers and smaller streams, provide important habitat for a wide variety of wildlife, in particular, for many species of wildfowl. Mute swans, grebes and herons are familiar sights on the waters across the region, as are kingfishers, bitterns, snipes and bearded tits. This abundance of wildlife is supported by more than 250 individual plant species, from the rare fen orchid to the common ragged robin. The Broads are also the last remaining haunt of the beautiful swallowtail butterfly which, with its three-inch wingspan, is Britain's largest.

Mute Swan

Bittern

Heron

Swallowtail

Kingfisher

Great Crested Grebe

Bearded Tit

Snipe

# RIVER BURE

The most northerly of the three main Broadland rivers, and also the longest, the Bure is now navigable from Coltishall Staithe to its junction with the River Yare, at Great Yarmouth. Rising at Melton Constable, near Aylsham, the busy and popular Bure has two tributaries, the River Thurne and the River Ant.

The picturesque setting of **Coltishall Staithe**, with its riverside pubs and excellent moorings, makes it a firm favourite with visitors. It lies a little way out of the village and runs along the pretty common.

Known as the 'Gateway to the Broads', the village of **Coltishall** lies a mile along the road from the staithe, and has a number of pretty cottages and a fine thatched church.

Set on a hill on the edge of the Bure Valley, **Belaugh** is a quiet little broadland village where the Church of St. Peter looks out over the staithe. It is well known for its fine example of a medieval painted rood screen. Nearby **Hoveton Hall Gardens** cover 15 acres of beautifully laid out gardens, and in the walled Spider Garden, with its colourful borders, stands this picturesque gardener's cottage.

Facing each other across the River Bure, **Wroxham** and Hoveton St. John are connected by a fine old road bridge, which was built in 1614 and is famously one of the most difficult to navigate on these waterways. Considered the 'Capital of the Broads', Wroxham was the first of the Broadland villages to cater for holiday-makers when a boatyard began to hire out yachts towards the end of the 19th century. Transport to Wroxham includes the delightful Bure Valley Railway, a narrow gauge steam railway which opened in 1990 and runs for nine miles starting at Aylsham.

Photo: Paul Douglas

About a mile south of Wroxham village is **Wroxham Broad**, home to the Norfolk Broads Yacht Club and the beautiful pleasure wherry 'Solace', which was built in 1903 at Reedham on the River Yare.

Surrounded by tranquil woodland and grassy banks, **Salhouse Broad** is a delightful quiet stretch of water with excellent moorings and opportunities for walks along well laid out nature trails.

At the little village of **Woodbastwick**, pretty thatched estate cottages line the traditional village green where the church of St. Fabian and St. Sebastian stands looking out to the thatched well-house. The elaborate village sign shows two woodcutters tying their leggings with 'bast', a pliable woody material extracted from lime trees, which gave the village its name. Woodbastwick also boasts its own local brewery, whose award-winning Wherry Bitter is served at the picturesque Fur & Feather pub.

A popular port of call for river goers, **Horning** is perhaps the prettiest of the riverside villages on the River Bure. Pubs, restaurants and cottages line the banks, along with a delightful village green, creating a bustling scene in the height of summer. The double-deck paddle steamer 'Southern Comfort' offers visitors river trips in style and was purpose built for sailing on the Broads.

Horning's picturesque Lower Street, with its pretty cottages, runs parallel to the river. Further along, at the ancient river crossing of Horning Ferry, stands this old weatherboarded wind pump, which was converted into a holiday home in the 1930s.

Divided into two parts by a thick bank, **Ranworth** is the largest of the broads in the Bure Valley. The village is accessed by a dyke from the River Bure, and the staithe is in fact situated on Malthouse Broad, so named after the old malthouses near the pub.

**Ranworth Staithe,** with its excellent moorings and modern facilities, is a favourite stopping off point, alive with craft of all descriptions. Close by are the village shop and pub, The Maltsters.

Celebrated as 'The Cathedral of the Broads', **Ranworth Church** holds the finest painted rood-screen in the country, and a remarkable medieval Latin songbook, known as the Ranworth Antiphoner. From the top of the church tower, there are fine panoramic views over Malthouse Broad and beyond.

The Inner Broad at Ranworth is a nature reserve, closed to navigation, where visitors are greeted by this pretty thatched floating information centre which has a fine viewing gallery looking out over the water. Malthouse Broad is a haven for sailing, and there are sailing tours of the lake aboard the 'Helen of Ranworth', which also operates as a ferry between the staithe and the Broads Wildlife Centre.

**South Walsham** village lies a mile from South Walsham Broad and contains a pretty village green and cottages. In the churchyard stands both the Church of St. Mary and the Church of St. Lawrence, although the latter is now used as a study centre. South Walsham Broad is connected to the River Bure by Fleet Dyke, and there is a delightful walk along the broad and dyke to the river and the ruins of St. Benet's Abbey.

A paradise for wildlife, **Fairhaven Woodland and Water Garden** lies by the privately owned Inner Broad at South Walsham, where three miles of scenic paths run through beautiful gardens and ancient woodland.

Situated in an isolated position, surrounded by grazing marshes, between the mouths of the Ant and Thurne, stand the remains of **St. Benet's Abbey**. Although the abbey was spared at the Dissolution of the Monasteries, all except the gatehouse was demolished shortly after, and a windmill was later built here.

After meeting the River Thurne at Thurne Mouth, the Bure takes a sharp turn and then passes through Upton Marshes on the way to Acle. At the end of Upton Dyke is the small staithe. Nearby **Upton** is one of the many small villages in the Broads which attract visitors to the area for their quiet picturesque charm.

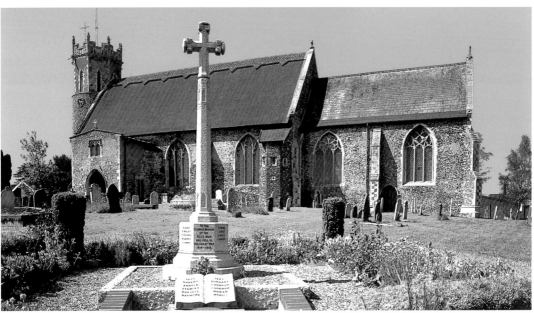

Once an important seaport, **Acle** is an attractive market town with an ancient thatched church, dating in part from Saxon times. Acle Bridge lies some way from the village and is famously believed to be haunted by the ghost of a local businessman who is said to have been murdered on the bridge.

A mile below Acle, on the northern shore of the river, **Stokesby** is a delightful village and a popular stopping off point before embarking on the final stretch of the waterway to Great Yarmouth. A short distance from the village is **Stracey Arms** with its fine drainage mill.

As the River Bure approaches **Great Yarmouth**, it joins the River Yare on its way to the sea. Always busy with leisure craft, the Yacht Station lies ten minutes' walk from the centre of town.

# RIVER ANT

Rising near North Walsham, the River Ant is navigable from Wayford Bridge and flows through some of the most enchanting scenery in Broadland, before joining the Bure, near St. Benet's Abbey. It is the shortest, and in places the narrowest, of the Broads rivers and its twisting, shallow route takes it through some beautiful towns and villages.

**Ludham Bridge**, with its excellent moorings, tea room, pub and boatyard, is always busy with boats and cruisers, and from here, there are walks with far-reaching views of Ludham and Potter Heigham Marshes Nature Reserve. It lies about a mile out of Ludham village itself, along the road to Horning.

On its way to **How Hill**, the River Ant passes graceful Turf Fen Mill, which was built in 1875 to drain Horning Marshes. A study centre has been set up at How Hill House, which stands surrounded by delightful Edwardian gardens and woodlands. The house looks down to the staithe and Boardman's Drainage Mill, while the old home of a marshman's family, Toad Hole Cottage is now a tiny museum.

Just south of Barton Broad is the peaceful village of **Irstead,** where lovely houses line the riverbanks. St. Michael's Church, with its thatched roof and sturdy tower, contains a number of noteworthy items including a 14th century font, a linenfold panelled pulpit and 14th century ironwork on the door.

Famously the place where a young Nelson learned to sail, **Barton Broad** is the second-largest of the Broads, consisting of more than 400 acres of open water, alder carr and fens. An ambitious restoration programme has improved this important wildlife habitat and brought back once lost landscape features and clear water. Barton Boardwalk offers an informative way to see the area and is the best viewpoint of this beautiful broad.

Photo: tournorfolk.co.uk

To the west of Barton Broad a dyke leads to **Neatishead**, a quiet little village which lies at the head of a wooded creek. Surrounded by delightful walks and pretty country lanes, the staithe provides fine moorings for small boats.

At the northern end of Barton Broad is the unspoilt little village of **Barton Turf** with its delightful village green, complete with a small pond and pretty cottages. The peaceful staithe has a large number of moorings and a boatyard, while nearby Barton Hall was once the home of Nelson's older sister, Catherine, and her husband.

**Gay's Staithe**, near Neatishead, has additional moorings for the many visitors to Barton Broad. From here, there are guided trips of the restored broad aboard the 'Ra', which is the country's first purpose-built passenger-carrying solar boat, launched by the Broads Authority in 2000.

At the northern edge of the Broads is **Stalham**, a small market town with a pretty church at one end of the high street. The staithe, with its boatyards and moorings, lies some way from the town and is home to the Museum of the Broads, which features fascinating displays exploring the relationship between people and nature.

The small staithe at **Sutton** offers a quieter place to moor, not far from Stalham. Standing near the entrance to Sutton Broad is **Hunsett Drainage Mill**, built in 1860 and restored around 1970. Further along, on the upper reaches of the River Ant, is the ancient crossing point of **Wayford Bridge**, where a low bridge carries the road over the river.

# RIVER THURNE

Rising near Martham Broad, the River Thurne is navigable from West Somerton. Flowing for just six miles through some of the most open countryside in the Broads, it is a wide river, ideal for sailing and boating. Near Thurne Mouth, where the Thurne joins the River Bure, stands the splendid drainage mill, known as St. Benet's Level Mill, which is still in full working order.

Marking the entrance to **Thurne** dyke and village, pretty white Thurne Mill, one of the most distinctive of the Broadland watermills, can be seen for miles. The dyke leads to the staithe where there are plenty of moorings overlooked by a number of pretty cottages.

**Womack Water** is a narrow waterway which branches off the River Thurne leading to the village of Ludham. The staithe is a lovely place to stop for a picnic and admire the heritage sailing fleet which is based here.

One of the major boating centres on the Broads is **Potter Heigham**, perhaps most famous for its medieval bridge which is notoriously difficult to navigate. A pilot is stationed here during the summer season to help small cruisers and yachts safely through this low-arched structure. The river is lined with hotels, shops and boatyards, as well as waterside bungalows, and from here, there is access to the Upper Thurne, Martham Broad, Hickling Broad and Horsey Mere.

A quiet little staithe leads from Martham Broad to the village of **West Somerton,** which is famously the birthplace of Robert Hales, who was known as the 'Norfolk Giant'. Born in 1820, he grew to a height of 7 feet 8 inches and was once presented to Queen Victoria.

**Martham** village lies halfway between the Norfolk Broads and the North Sea. Its lovely pond is overlooked by some pretty thatched cottages and the Kings' Arms. Ferrygate Lane leads to tranquil **Martham Dyke**, which is lined on both sides by public footpaths and fine moorings.

At **Hickling**, the Pleasure Boat Inn gives its name to the dyke which runs off the northern end of Hickling Broad. The popular pub dates back, in part, to the 17th century and has moorings at its doorstep.

Photo: tournorfolk.co.uk

**Hickling Broad** is the largest of all the broads, a vast, shallow expanse of water, fringed by reeds. Designated a National Nature Reserve and in the care of Norfolk Wildlife Trust, there is a visitors' centre, observation towers, bird hides and viewing platforms from where to enjoy the large variety of wildlife which can be seen here.

A favourite with photographers and artists, these charming thatched boathouses stand at Hickling Broad, blending perfectly into the scenery.

Photo: tournorfolk.co.uk

A beautifully restored five-storey windpump, **Horsey Mill** was built in 1912 and is now owned by The National Trust. Open to the public, there are magnificent views across **Horsey Mere** and to the coast from the top of the mill, which continued to work until 1943 when it was severely damaged by lightning.

The closest of the Broadland villages to the sea, **Horsey** has a number of pretty cottages set in leafy country lanes. Its peaceful Church of All Saints is one of many Norfolk churches which features a rounded tower, here topped by an octagonal bell tower, thought to date from around 1220.

**Horsey Dyke** is a popular mooring place, not least due to the picture postcard view of Horsey Windpump in all its glory. Derelict **Brograve Drainage Mill**, which is perched on the banks of the Waxham New Cut, north of Horsey Mere, was built in 1771 by Sir Berney Brograve.

# RIVER YARE

Rising near East Dereham, 15 miles west of Norwich, the River Yare extends for over 55 miles on its way to the sea. Beautiful **Berney Arms Mill** stands by the entrance to **Breydon Water**, a vast tidal broad which is the confluence of the Rivers Bure, Yare and Waveney. The tall mill was built around 1870 to grind a constituent of cement, and it remained in use as a drainge mill until 1951.

Photo: tournorfolk.co.uk

Photo: tournorfolk.co.uk

At **Reedham**, a ferry carries passengers and vehicles across the river at the only crossing point between Great Yarmouth and Norwich. Today, worked by a motorised chain system, it was once wound by hand.

Photo: Paul Douglas

A small tributary, the River Chet enters the Yare between Cantley and Reedham, and gives access to the market town of **Loddon**. At one time, traditional wherries were a common sight on the River Chet as they carried goods to Loddon Mill. Close to where the two rivers join is Norton Marsh Drainage Mill, built in 1863 and fitted with a new boat-shaped cap in 1997. Today, Loddon is a tranquil town with a number of beautiful riverside properties overlooking the popular staithe.

Photo: tournorfolk.co.uk

Photo: Daniel Tink

Beautiful **Rockland Broad** is connected to the River Yare by two dykes, the Short Dyke and the Fleet Dyke. The long distance footpath known as Wherryman's Way winds past this peaceful hamlet and over the nearby marshes, reed beds and grazing meadows.

Photo: Daniel Tink

Two miles from Rockland, surrounded by open country, is the busy boating centre of **Brundall** with its boatyards, marina and local sailing club.

The Great Broad at **Whitlingham Country Park** is one of the first broads to have been created for centuries and now provides new habitats for wildlife.

A tributary of the River Yare, the Wensum flows through the heart of **Norwich**, dividing the city in two. A riverside path follows the course of the river and offers delightful glimpses of the city, while the tree-lined yacht station provides moorings only a few minutes walk from the cathedral.

# RIVER WAVENEY

Rising at Redgrave Fen, the River Waveney is navigable from Geldeston Lock to Breydon Water, near Great Yarmouth. The most southerly of the main rivers in the Broads, it forms the border between Norfolk and Suffolk for most of its length, as it passes through the towns of Diss, Bungay and Beccles.

Overlooking the Halvergate Marshes is **Burgh Castle**, one of a chain of forts built by the Romans to defend the east coast against Saxon invaders. The local parish church is dedicated to St. Peter and St. Paul and it is one of the 124 round-tower churches in Norfolk.

**St. Olaves** is a welcome stopping off point on this very flat section of the Broads. The village has a nice riverside pub and a short walk away are the ruins of the Augustinian Priory of St. Olaves and St. Mary.

**Somerleyton Hall**, a splendid Victorian mansion, was built in the Anglo-Italian style around the shell of an earlier Tudor and Jacobean house. The state rooms at Somerleyton Hall contain fine paintings and carvings, while in the gardens, little has changed since Victorian times.

Connected to the River Waveney by a dyke, **Oulton Broad** forms the southern gateway to the Broads and is a popular yachting centre always crowded with pleasure craft. On its northern shore stands a large converted brewery, while nearby is the picturesque Nicholas Everitt Park. A lock at the eastern end takes boats through to Lake Lothing, which in turn gives access to the sea.

As the river widens out near the town of **Beccles**, it provides good opportunities for sailing. The centre of the town is a conservation area with many buildings of historic interest. St. Michael's Parish Church stands in a commanding position overlooking the valley, and from the top of the bell tower, there are delightful views of the Waveney, as it winds through the town and the surrounding countryside.

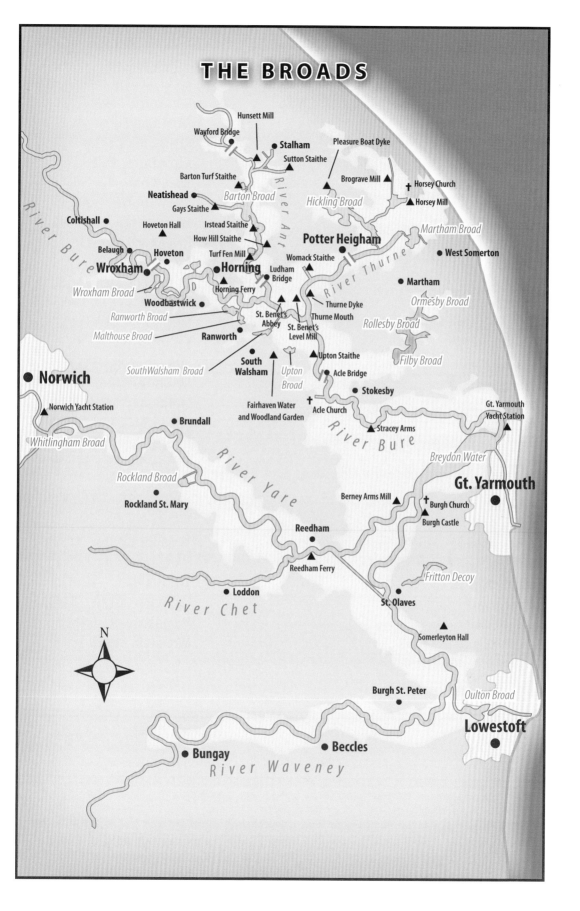

# THE BROADS

Hunsett Mill
Wayford Bridge
Stalham
Pleasure Boat Dyke
Sutton Staithe
Barton Turf Staithe
Brograve Mill
Horsey Church
Neatishead
Barton Broad
Horsey Mill
Gays Staithe
Hickling Broad
Coltishall
Hoveton Hall
Irstead Staithe
Martham Broad
Belaugh
How Hill Staithe
Potter Heigham
West Somerton
Hoveton
Turf Fen Mill
Womack Staithe
Wroxham
Horning
Martham
Ludham Bridge
Wroxham Broad
Horning Ferry
Ormesby Broad
Woodbastwick
Thurne Dyke
Rollesby Broad
Ranworth Broad
St. Benet's Abbey
Thurne Mouth
Malthouse Broad
St. Benet's Level Mill
Filby Broad
Ranworth
Upton Staithe
South Walsham
Acle Bridge
Norwich
SouthWalsham Broad
Upton Broad
Stokesby
Norwich Yacht Station
Fairhaven Water and Woodland Garden
Acle Church
Gt. Yarmouth Yacht Station
Whitlingham Broad
Brundall
River Bure
Breydon Water
Rockland Broad
Berney Arms Mill
Gt. Yarmouth
Rockland St. Mary
Burgh Church
Burgh Castle
Reedham
River Yare
Fritton Decoy
Reedham Ferry
Loddon
St. Olaves
River Chet
Somerleyton Hall
N
Burgh St. Peter
Oulton Broad
Lowestoft
Bungay
Beccles
River Waveney

River Bure
River Ant
River Thurne

# INDEX

Acle  20
Barton Broad  27
Barton Turf Staithe  28
Beccles  46
Belaugh  7
Berney Arms  40
Breydon Water  40
Brograve Mill  39
Brundall  42
Burgh Castle  44
Coltishall  6
Fairhaven Water and Woodland Garden  19
Gay's Staithe  29
Great Yarmouth Yacht Station  21
Hickling  3, 37
Horning  12–13
Horsey  38–39
Hoveton Hall Gardens  7
How Hill  25
Hunsett Mill  31
Irstead  26
Loddon  41
Ludham Bridge  22–23
Martham  36
Neatishead  28
Norwich Yacht Station  43
Oulton Broad  46
Potter Heigham  34–35

Ranworth  14–17
Reedham Ferry  41
River Ant  22–31
River Bure  6–21
River Chet  41
River Thurne  32–39
River Waveney  44–46
River Yare  40–43
Rockland Broad  42
St. Benet's Abbey  18, 19
St. Benet's Level Mill  2, 32
St. Olaves  45
Salhouse Broad  10
Somerleyton Hall  45
South Walsham  2, 18
Stalham  30
Stokesby  21
Stracey Arms  21
Sutton Staithe  31
Thurne  32–33
Turf Fen Mill  24–25
Upton Staithe  20
Wayford Bridge  31
West Somerton  36
Whitlingham  42
Womack Staithe  32–33
Woodbastwick  10
Wroxham  8–10

First published in the United Kingdom in 2010
by J. Salmon Ltd., 100 London Road, Sevenoaks, Kent TN13 1BB

Copyright © J. Salmon Ltd.

Printed in the United Kingdom by J. Salmon Ltd.
ISBN 978-1-84640-244-9
Code: 12/05/30/01

Front cover: **Horsey Mill**      Inside front cover: **River Ant at How Hill**      Title page: **Thurne Mill and Dyke**
Inside back cover: **St. Benet's Level Mill**      Back cover: **River Ant**